Reptiles

Horned Lizards

by Lyn A. Sirota

Consulting Editor: Gail Saunders-Smith, PhD

Content Consultants: Joe Maierhauser, President/CEO
Terry Phillip, Curator of Reptiles
Reptile Gardens, Rapid City, South Dakota

Capstone
press®

Mankato, Minnesota

Pebble Plus is published by Capstone Press,
151 Good Counsel Drive, P.O. Box 669, Mankato, Minnesota 56002.
www.capstonepress.com

Library of Congress Cataloging-in-Publication Data
Sirota, Lyn A., 1963–
    Horned lizards / by Lyn A. Sirota.
    p. cm. — (Pebble plus. Reptiles)
    Includes bibliographical references and index.
    Summary: "Simple text and photographs present horned lizards,
how they look, where they live, and what they do" — Provided by publisher.
    ISBN 13: 978-1-4296-3318-5 (library binding)
    1. Horned toads — Juvenile literature. I. Title.
SF459.L5S574 2010
597.95'4 — dc22
                                         2009000044

Editorial Credits
Jenny Marks, editor; Matt Bruning, designer; Svetlana Zhurkin, media researcher

Photo Credits
Nature Picture Library/Barry Mansell, 13
Peter Arnold/John Cancalosi, 7, 15, 17
Photolibrary/age fotostock/John Cancalosi, 11
Shutterstock/Brad Phillips, 9; Derek L. Miller, 5; Eugene Buchko, 21; PhotoD, back cover, 1
Tom Stack & Associates/Joe McDonald, front cover

Note to Parents and Teachers

The Reptiles set supports science standards related to life science. This book describes and
illustrates horned lizards. The images support early readers in understanding the text. The
repetition of words and phrases helps early readers learn new words. This book also introduces
early readers to subject-specific vocabulary words, which are defined in the Glossary section.
Early readers may need assistance to read some words and to use the Table of Contents,
Glossary, Read More, Internet Sites, and Index sections of the book.

Table of Contents

Crowned Reptile

Horned lizards are

short, wide reptiles.

Some people call them

horny toads,

but they are really lizards.

Horned lizards have crowns
on the backs of their heads.
These long, pointed scales
look like horns.

Fourteen different kinds

of horned lizards

live in North America.

They are from 2 to 8 inches

(5 to 20 centimeters) long.

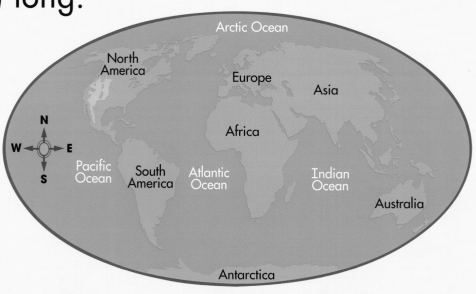

where horned lizards live

Lizard Living

Horned lizards sit in the sun
to keep warm.
They rest under the sand
to cool off.

Horned lizards eat ants.

They swallow hundreds

of them whole.

Spiders are a good dessert.

Snakes, hawks, and coyotes
hunt horned lizards.
If predators are near,
lizards puff up their bodies.
They look too big to eat.

Horned lizards scare off predators in other ways. They hiss and shoot blood from their eyes.

A Horned Lizard's Life

Some kinds of horned lizards

give birth to live young.

Other kinds lay eggs.

A horned lizard clutch

has 24 to 36 eggs.

Horned Lizard Life Cycle

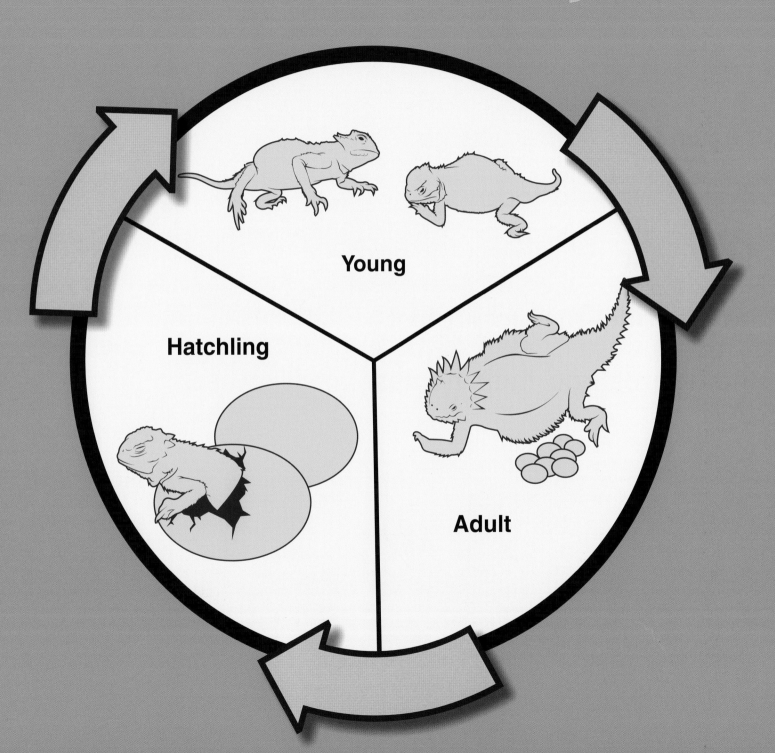

Young

Hatchling

Adult

Fewer horned lizards
live in the wild today.
Texas and other states
have made laws to protect
the lizards and their homes.

Glossary

clutch — a group of eggs laid by a single female lizard

hiss — to make an "sss" sound like a snake

predator — an animal that hunts other animals for food

protect — to keep safe

scale — one of many small pieces of hard skin

toad — an amphibian that looks like a frog but has rougher, drier skin

Read More

Bredeson, Carmen. *Fun Facts about Lizards!* I Like Reptiles and Amphibians! Berkeley, N.J.: Enslow Elementary, 2008.

Haskins, Lori. *Bloody Horned Lizards*. Gross-Out Defenses. New York: Bearport Pub., 2009.

Murray, Julie. *Lizards*. Animal Kingdom. Edina, Minn.: Abdo, 2005.

Internet Sites

FactHound offers a safe, fun way to find Internet sites related to this book. All of the sites on FactHound have been researched by our staff.

Here's all you do:

Visit *www.facthound.com*

FactHound will fetch the best sites for you!

Index

Word Count: 171
Grade: 1
Early-Intervention Level: 20